Katahdin, Baxter State Park,
by Paul A. Knaut Jr.

MAINE ✒ Four Seasons

MAINE

✒ Four Seasons

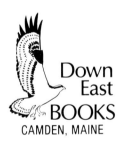

Down
East
BOOKS
CAMDEN, MAINE

*Left — Great Blue Heron, Islesboro,
by Harold Hammond*

MAINE – Four Seasons

Copyright © 1973 by Down East Enterprise, Inc.

Library of Congress Catalog Card No. 73-86683
ISBN 0-89272-009-3

Acadia National Park, Mount Desert Island, by Marie Ivey Menzietti.
Ocean Drive, Mount Desert Island, by Marie Ivey Menzietti.

From **MAINE PARADISE** by Russell D. Butcher and Marie Ivey Menzietti
Copyright © 1973 by Russell D. Butcher and Marie Ivey Menzietti
All rights reserved
Reprinted by permission of The Viking Press, Inc.

The Spite House Garden, Rockport, by Vivian Dow.
The Spite House, Rockport, by Vivian Dow.

Courtesy of Mr. & Mrs. Donald D. Dodge.

Along the Carabasset River, by R. Oliver Post.
Back Cover - North Edgecomb, by R. Oliver Post.

Courtesy of Northeast Banks of Maine.

Designed by J. D. Parker.

SUMMER

Camden
Harbor
by
Dick Smith

West Penobscot Bay, by Harold Hammond

Schooner "Timberwind," Rockport Harbor,
by Yapa

Spinnaker Run,
Monhegan Race,
by Gardner Roberts

Internationals racing
off Mount Desert Island,
by Rosalinda R. Madara

Schoodic Surf,
by Robert Hylander

Penobscot Bay and the Camden Hills from Sedgwick, by Jeremy Dickson

Reid State Park, by Herbert P. Detjens

Photos by Martin Meltz

Tidal pool
on shore of Flint Island, Harrington,
by Jeremy Dickson

Portland Head Light,
by Dick Smith

Five Islands,
by Roche

Pemaquid Light,
by George French

Photos by William K. Sacco

Above and right – Isle au Haut, Penobscot Bay, by John R. Dice

Union Congregational Church, Isle au Haut, by John R. Dice

Pemaquid Point Light,
by Dick Smith

Garden at The Spite House, Rockport, by George Taloumis.
Courtesy of Mr. and Mrs. Donald D. Dodge

Garden of Mrs. Lewis A. Garland, Eden, Maine,
by Roche

The Spite House garden, Rockport, by Vivian Dow,
courtesy of Mr. and Mrs. Donald D. Dodge

The Spite House, Rockport, by Vivian Dow,
courtesy of Mr. and Mrs. Donald D. Dodge

Photos by Wilma A. Huntley

Five Islands, by Charles Tinkham

Newborn fawn, Bethel, by Lee H. Hutchins

Cobscook, by Era S. VanDenburg

FALL

Trout fishing, Baxter State Park,
by Nelson Groffman

*Tidal marsh,
by Roche*

*Ocean Drive,
Acadia
National Park,
Brad Vogel*

Kezar Lake,
by
F. Lucille Johnstone

Lobstermen at
Round Pound, by
Douglas Armsden

Monhegan Island,
by Yapa

Last Haying, by G. Lewis Johnson

Schoodic Point, Acadia National Park,
by Robert Holland

Near Bridgton, by Nelson Groffman

Artists' Bridge, Newry,
by George French

Near Appleton, by Vivian Dow

West Cumberland, by F. Lucille Johnstone

By Bud Yallalee

Fall color, Yarmouth, by Herbert Detjens

Near Andover,
by Harold E. Hammond

Lorimer Chapel,
Colby College, Waterville,
by Earl Smith

Photos by Vivian Dow

The sweep of autumn, by Kip Brundage

*Along the
Carrabasset
River,
by R. Oliver Post*

Mount Desert Island, by Charles Laffin

WINTER

By James Gibson

By James Gibson

Camden Harbor, by R. Oliver Post

By James Gibson

Pemaquid Light, by Patrick Sekerak

Mt. Battie,
by R. Oliver Post

Winter in
North Haven,
by Elliott Beveridge

By Vivian Dow

ooners at Wiscasset, by R. B. Laughlin

Yarmouth, by Herbert P. Detjens

Bridgton,
by David Witham

Near Bridgton, by Carleton W. Patriquin

By Peter H. Burbank

Tree Sparrow, by R. Waldo Tyler

*East Fryeburg landscape,
by Carleton Patriquin*

By Ralph H. Crowell

Waterford, by Dick Smith

Snow Bowl Ski Area, Camden, by R. Oliver Post

Lobster traps on Wharf Hill, Monhegan, by Richard Farrell

Mud Pond
Stream,
Allagash
Region,
by
Michael Bond

Photo by
Peter H. Burbank

Mt. Katahdin,
by Paul A. Knaut Jr.

Sandy River,
by Paul A. Knaut Jr.

SPRING

Rhodora in bloom,
by Paul A. Knaut Jr.

Painted trillium,
by Wilma A. Huntley

By Vivian Dow

Maiden Cliff Trail,
Camden,
by David Jinno

By William E. Hebden

Violets,
by Maxwell L. Rollins

Lady's Slippers, by Vivian Dow

*Katahdin
Falls,
Appalachian Trail,
by Paul A. Knaut Jr.*

The Bull Branch, Sunday River, by Vincent DeFelice

Roaring Brook,
Baxter
State Park,
by
James E. Christie

*First
Congregational
Church,
Searsport,
by
Maxwell Rollins*

ft –
enceforth,”
ne of
s. Alberta Hitchcock,
eepscot,
William Searle

By Vivian Dow

Baldwin, by O. B. Denison

Right – Oak Hill, Scarborough, by Scott Lovejoy

By Robert M. Hyde

Spice bush,
Belfast,
by
Vivian Dow

Sprucehead, by Marny Emanuel

Sunrise over
Highland Lake, Bridgton,
by David A. Bast

*On Cadillac
Mountain,
Mount Desert
Island,
by
Charles Laffin*

*Monhegan
Island,
by
Ruth Lewis*

Spring outfitting,
Kittery Point,
by Douglas Armsden

By Herbert Douglas

Monhegan window garden, by Yapa

Mouth of the Kennebec River, by Stephen T. Whitney

Bernard, by W. H. Ballard

By W. C. Roemer

Spinnaker Run, by Herbert Detjens

Ocean Drive, Mount Desert Island, by Marie Ivey Menzietti

Sunset, Pulpit Harbor, North Haven, by David Dean Crofoot

Brown's Head, Muscongus Bay, by John McKee

By Paul A. Knaut Jr.